MALLETS, CHISELS & PLANES

THE BUILDING OF THE TALL SHIP
KALMAR NYCKEL
FROM VISION TO LAUNCH

First Edition

Published by Cedar Tree Books, Ltd.
Nine Germay Drive, Wilmington, Delaware 19804

ISBN: 1-892142-19-8

Editor: Phil Maggitti
Design: Christine Celano Graphic Design, Wilmington, Delaware
Photography: Chris Queeney except pages: 26, 31, 36, 37, 39, 44, 51, and 62
by J.N. Peters and the Kalmar Nyckel Foundation
Illustrations pages 9 and 14: Courtesy of the Historical Society of Delaware

Copyright © 2003 Cedar Tree Books, Ltd.

Library of Congress Cataloging-in-Publication Data
Ireland, Charles E. Jr., 1935-
Mallets, Chisels & Planes : The Building of the Tall Ship Kalmar
Nyckel from Vision to Launch / Charles E. Ireland, Jr. – 1st ed. p. cm.
ISBN: 1-892142-19-8 (alk. paper)
1. Kalmar Nyckel (Ship)–Design and construction.
2. Kalmar Nyckel (Ship : Replica)–Design and construction. 1. Title.
VM395.K34174 2003
623.8´22–dc21   2003053214

ALL RIGHTS RESERVED
No part of this book may be reproduced in any manner
without the express written consent of the publisher, except in
the case of brief excerpts in critical reviews and articles.

Set in Bembo and Trajan
Printed by CS Graphics Pte., Ltd., Singapore, on acid free paper.

MALLETS, CHISELS & PLANES

THE BUILDING OF THE TALL SHIP
KALMAR NYCKEL
FROM VISION TO LAUNCH

CHARLES E. IRELAND, JR.

CEDAR TREE BOOKS, LTD.

TRIBUTE TO WOODEN BOATS

"Wooden boats...are alive, wooden boats...have a soul."

"All wooden boats are beautiful, as if the grace of the forest trees were bequeathed in abundance to every plank sawn."

"I truly believe that wooden boats have a lot to teach us about our purpose on the planet."

Jon Wilson,
founder and editor in chief *WoodenBoat* magazine,
from the book *Wooden Boats: In
Pursuit of the Perfect Craft at an American Boatyard*
by Michael Ruhlman

FOR MY DAUGHTERS KATHLEEN AND LISA
AND GRANDCHILDREN
GREGORY, MARCUS, KELLY, CAITLIN AND KRISTINE
AS WELL AS FOR
WOODEN BOAT BUILDERS EVERYWHERE

THE ORIGINAL KALMAR NYCKEL

A BRIEF HISTORY

Although no drawings of the original Kalmar Nyckel exist today and her fate is not exactly clear, much is known of her distinguished career as merchant vessel, warship and explorer. She was built in Holland in the late 1620s. She was classified as a Dutch pinnace, meaning she was a medium-size, three-masted, square-rigged, armed merchant ship. The Dutch built many of this class of ship, and their configuration, specifications and appearance are well documented. It was from such documentation and careful review of seventeenth-century marine carving and ship decorations that plans and drawings for the new Kalmar Nyckel were made.

Her recorded history begins in 1629 when she was purchased by the Swedish cities of Kalmar and Jonkoping. She was named Kalmar Nyckel meaning "Key of Kalmar," and along with land-based forts became part of the cities' coastal defense system.

In June 1637 the Swedish Crown ordered the preparation of two ships for a trade and colonization voyage to the New World. The Kalmar Nyckel and the smaller Fogel Grip were chosen. After a disastrous start in the fall of 1637, when both ships were storm damaged in the North Sea, they limped into Holland for repairs. They resumed their voyage again on December 31, 1637, and arrived at The Rocks on the banks of the Christina River on March 29, 1638. There a small band of settlers established the colony of New Sweden and built a fort called Christina. The Kalmar Nyckel would make three more voyages to help supply and populate the growing colony.

Seventeenth-century shipbuilding records and review of representative period woodcarvings resulted in development of specifications, plans and drawings from which the new Kalmar Nyckel was built.

Her second voyage, in April, 1640, brought her again to The Rocks. After supplies, trade goods and additional settlers were offloaded, she took on a cargo of furs and other articles of trade and set sail for home a month later.

On her third voyage to Fort Christina in New Sweden she was joined by the freight ship Charitas (Charity). They arrived in November 1641 and departed that same month with very little cargo, since competition and inroads by the English had severely curtailed the fur trade. They sailed for France and there took on a cargo of salt before returning to Sweden in April 1642.

On her fourth and last voyage to Fort Christina the Kalmar Nyckel and the Fama (Fame) left Sweden in December 1643 and arrived in New Sweden in February 1644. On returning to Sweden the Kalmar Nyckel was commissioned by the admiralty to serve as a warship in a conflict with Denmark.

By May 1645 the Kalmar Nyckel was rigged for battle and served Sweden as a scout ship because she was known to be fast and maneuverable. She survived an engagement with the Danish warship St. Peter on August 8, 1645, and with the end of the war there were thoughts of her making yet another voyage to New Sweden with provisions and soldiers. However, she was now quite old and upon inspection was not deemed sufficiently seaworthy for a fifth crossing.

On June 19, 1651, Queen Christina authorized the sale of the Kalmar Nyckel to a Cornelius Rolofsson, and, unfortunately, here the record ends. Mr. Rolofsson's nationality and intended use for the Kalmar Nyckel are not known, but in later years there is a record in Holland of a ship thought to be the old Kalmar Nyckel. That ship was sunk in a battle with the English.

Regardless of her end the Kalmar Nyckel had a remarkable record of four transatlantic voyages in her twenty-two years of service to Sweden. Ships of the seventeenth-century usually had relatively short lives. The Kalmar Nyckel's longevity was extraordinary and a tribute to her construction and the skill of her building crew.

Manuscript map of the original settlements on the Delaware River and Bay, hand-colored by Benjamin Ferris, early nineteenth-century. Ferris materials, library collections, Historical Society of Delaware.

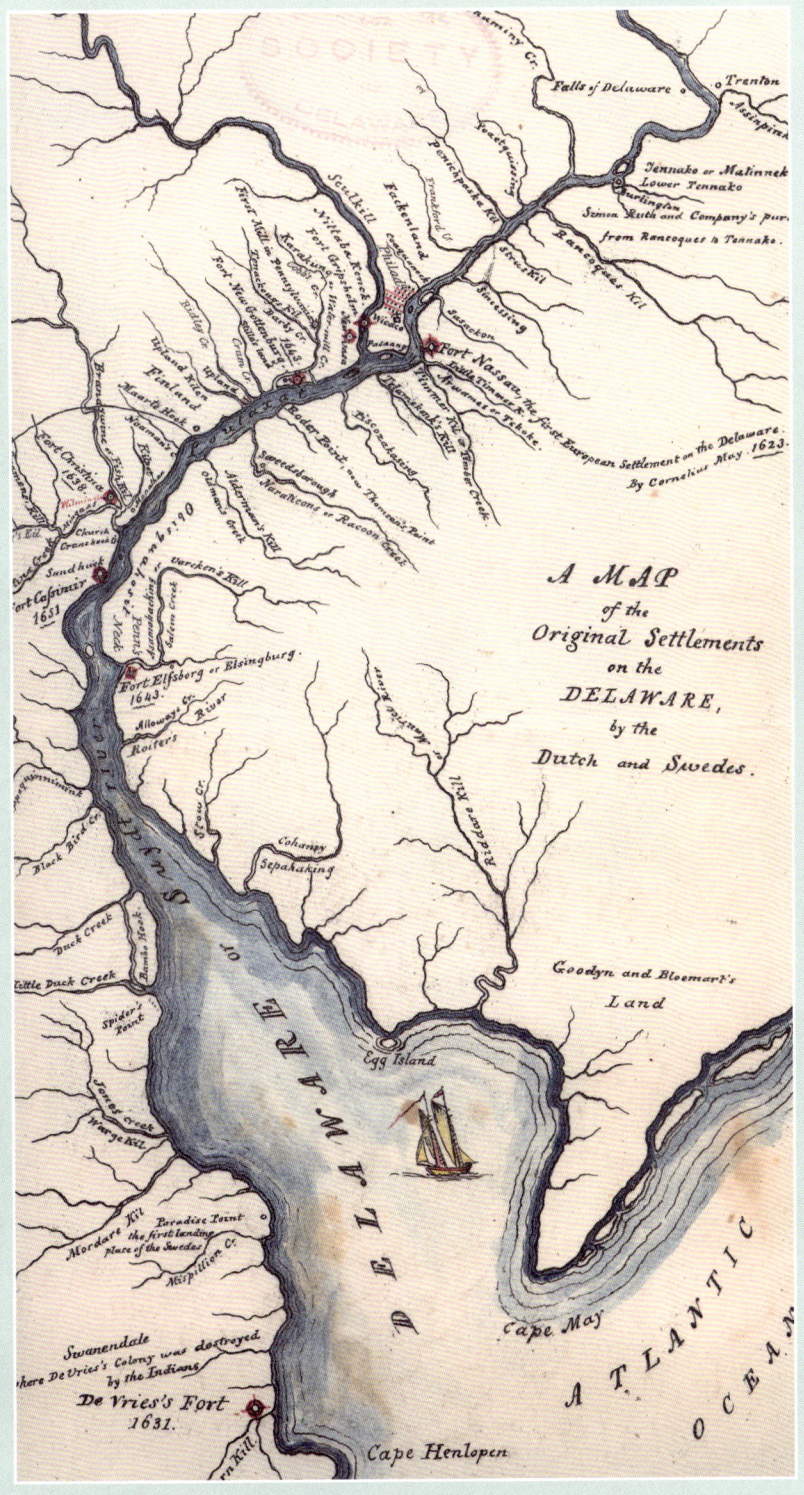

FOREWORD

Dreamers dream dreams, and craftsmen make things with their hands and hearts. When dreamers and craftsmen come together, visions take shape and dreams are born.

This is the story of the dream of a tall ship reborn. It traces the building and rebirth of the Kalmar Nyckel, a seventeenth-century Swedish-owned, Dutch-built pinnace. The ship has a unique place in the history of the Swedish colonization of the Delaware Valley. The story is written from the perspective of a volunteer member of the crew that built the new Kalmar Nyckel. It is as much about the people, the skills, the crafts and the emotions, that are the heart and soul of wooden-boat building, as the ship itself.

Wooden-boat building is an art made up of the vision, talent and skill of those who share the dream of a stout vessel designed and built to challenge the elements of wind, weather and sea. It is a symphony of sight, sound, smell and emotion: the sight of a perfect joint, a fair line, a graceful hull, fire, smoke, steam and sparks; the sound of anvil, hammer, saw, mallet, chisel, plane, and the voices and accents of men and women at work; the smell of fish oil and turpentine, oakum, tar, wood, canvas and the sweat of honest work; the emotions of love, joy and pride.

This book is dedicated to all the volunteers, artisans and craftsmen who helped make the Kalmar Nyckel dream come true and to young students of early American and Delaware history.

For additional information about the Kalmar Nyckel and the foundation that supports her, log on to www.kalnyc.org. For photographs of the Kalmar Nyckel and other tall ships as well as examples of work by some of the artisans who worked on the Kalmar Nyckel, visit www.seafoto.com.

The dream of a tall ship reborn takes shape as shipwright, Joel Welter guides the placement of one of the ship's hand carved sculptures.

MALLETS, CHISELS & PLANES

THE BUILDING OF THE TALL SHIP
KALMAR NYCKEL
FROM VISION TO LAUNCH

14

MALLETS, CHISELS & PLANES

MALLETS, CHISELS & PLANES

In November 1637 a ship called Kalmar Nyckel, meaning "Key of Kalmar," set sail with her sister ship, the Fogel Grip, from Gothenburg, Sweden, bound for the New World with a cargo of trade goods and a small but courageous band of soldiers, sailors and twenty-four settlers. The ships encountered rough weather in the North Sea, and both were damaged. After repairs and provisioning in Holland, they set out again on December 31, 1637. Three months later, on March 29, 1638, the ships arrived on the banks of the Christina River at a place called The Rocks. Here the settlers built a fort and trading post called Christina in honor of Sweden's young queen and founded the colony of New Sweden. It was the first successful European settlement in the Delaware Valley, and it took root and prospered on a site that much later would be part of the city of Wilmington, Delaware. The little colony grew and expanded throughout much of the Delaware Valley until it was taken over by the Dutch in 1655. Between 1638 and 1643 the Kalmar Nyckel was to make four round trips from Sweden to Fort Christina, a record unmatched by any other New World colonial vessel.

In 1986, nearly 350 years later, a few men and women with a vision gathered to share their dream of one day reconstructing the Kalmar Nyckel. But where, how and who would build her? Their dream, like all good dreams, was a very big one indeed—reconstruct the Kalmar Nyckel as close to the original as possible, using as many of the seventeenth-century ship-building skills, tools and methods as they could. That meant research, plans, materials, volunteers, artisans, tools, a building crew, a master shipbuilder and money. In short, mallets, chisels and planes and the knowledge, talent, skills and hearts of dedicated craftsmen, volunteers and financial backers—a tall order for a tall ship!

Landing at The Rocks on March 29, 1638 *from Amandus Johnson,* The Swedish Settlements on the Delaware: 1638-1664. Volume 1, *(Philadelphia: 1911). Courtesy of the Historical Society of Delaware.*

When we dream good dreams, almost anything is possible. And so it was with this dream.

Some old shipyard property on the banks of the Christiana River, very close to where the original Kalmar Nyckel landed in 1638, was found, and a seventeenth-century-style shipyard was built with the help of volunteers and donated materials. A master shipbuilder and his wife helped attract a building crew made up of volunteers, shipwrights, blacksmiths, wood carvers, sail makers, caulkers and riggers from near and far.

Before long a building crew was at work in the little shipyard. Men with names like Olaf, Uwe, Christer, Joel, Roger, Lytton, John, Jim, Thacker, Patrick, Steve, Dick, Ron, Miklos, Rich and many more. Women with names like Kelly, Liz, Olga, Kisa, Peg and Cindy. Some were known by their given names; others by "shipyard names" such as "Squirrel," "Rainbow," "Deetles," "Woody," "Joe DeCaulka (Joe the Caulker)," "Bopper," "Little Don," "Big Don" and, of course, "Middle Don."

Dream builders, master shipbuilder Allen Rawl and wife Liz managed the project from start to finish with loving care and meticulous attention to authenticity and detail..

They came from Sweden, Denmark, Germany, Canada, Maryland, Massachusetts, California, Maine, Pennsylvania, Iowa, Texas, West Virginia, New York, Virginia, Rhode Island, Connecticut, Oklahoma, Minnesota, New Jersey and Delaware. Each had a needed skill and a desire to be part of something special: a piece of history in the making; history in the shape of a wooden tall ship—the new Kalmar Nyckel!

A bustling little shipyard was built from scratch on the banks of the Christina River very close to where the original Kalmar Nyckel landed in 1638.

Soon the symphony of the sights, sounds, smells and emotions of wooden-boat building filled the little shipyard as it fairly hummed with anticipation and activity. With schedules to keep and deadlines to meet, there was no time to lose! There was a ship to build!

As the shipyard was being readied, the master shipbuilder personally selected trees from the rain forests of Central America and the Pacific Northwest for the wood that would become the new Kalmar Nyckel. Wood was chosen for its special properties of strength, weight, grain, resistance to rot or ease of working as well as for its intended use and place on the ship. Heavy, dense woods became the hull and other hard-working parts. Lighter but strong wood was fashioned into bitts, masts, yards and decking, and carvers used a variety of straight grained and easily worked woods for the structural and decorative carvings that would grace the ship.

There were purpleheart, greenheart and locust for strength and resistance to the effects of salt, sea and weather. These woods were used for the hull and planking and for the ship's many blocks that help raise, lower and position the sails. Other rain forest woods with strange names included black cabbage bark, Billy Webb, Cortez, mora and sapodilla.

Douglas fir, yellow pine, and Sitka spruce from Washington, Oregon and Alaska were selected for strength and light weight. These woods became masts, yards, spars, bitts and deck planks.

Mahogany, Atlantic white cedar, western red cedar, locust, oak and fir were all used by the carvers. What they were carving and how it would be used on the ship determined the best wood for the job. Purely decorative pieces were carved of mahogany and cedar. Functional pieces that had ship's work to do, such as bitts, knees, chocks, and fairleads, would be carved from locust, Douglas fir or oak.

Finally, tamarack larch (hack-ma-tack) from New England was used to fashion the more than two hundred knees that give the ship strength and stability in heavy seas and rough weather. This wood is strong and hard and forms a rigid right angle or natural knee with curved grain where a branch or root met the tree trunk. When made into a ship's knee, the wood grain follows the angle, which makes a very strong structural brace.

A hack-ma-tack knee waiting to become one of over 200 horizontal and vertical braces used to give the ship exceptional strength and stability.

Now the dream was beginning to take shape! There was a plan, a master shipbuilder, a shipyard, shipwrights, a big pile of wood and growing support for the project.

Work days at the shipyard started at sunrise and ended at sunset. Shipwrights began arriving for work before first light. Some lived at the shipyard in a dormitory over the tool shed. Others came on foot, by bicycle or in a variety of cars, vans and trucks, many of which were very well traveled indeed and carried the dings, dents and scars of other shipyards in other distant places.

Like gypsies, shipwrights take their special skills wherever wooden boats are being built. A duffel bag for clothes, mostly of the work variety, a stout box for the tools of their craft and a reasonably reliable means to get from place to place are all they need to work their magic with wood, iron, cloth and rope.

With the first streaks of light painting the eastern sky, the shipwrights would gather in the tool shed where the coffee was always strong and hot. Here they would get their work assignments, collect their tools and swap stories or get advice on how to measure, cut or fit a piece of the puzzle that would one day be a magnificent tall ship.

Outside in the yard, where the ship would take shape, all was peaceful. The only sounds were the cries of sea gulls wheeling overhead and the occasional creak and groan of great timbers that would soon be transformed as if by magic into a tall ship.

Each workday the symphony of shipyard sights, sounds and smells began at first light. Here a shipwright adds his notes to the timeless concert of wooden boat building.

When the sun cleared the horizon, there could be heard the first tentative but unmistakable thunk of a trunnel being driven home, the muted whine of a saw or the tap of a mallet. Great puffs of black smoke billowing from the blacksmith's chimney signaled that the blacksmith was poking and prodding her embers to life for another day of turning iron bars into functional works of art. As the sun rose higher, the yard began to ring with the time-honored and wonderful sounds of wooden-boat building. The symphony of shipbuilding sights, sounds and smells soon merged with, and then overpowered, the sea gull's song and the creaking quiet of the little shipyard at first light. The scent of fresh-brewed coffee, sawdust, fish oil, turpentine and the blacksmith's glowing coals drifted in the early morning air, mixing with the musky scent of the nearby river and tidal flats as the little shipyard awakened to another busy work day.

The same workday symphony was repeated day after day and seemed to follow the sun's path across the sky, rising to its full voice at midday and then gradually diminishing as the sun moved lower toward the western horizon. It was as if the sun was conducting an orchestra of shipwrights playing the instruments of their trade—mallets, chisels and planes.

With the setting sun the sea gull's song could again be heard, accompanied by the creaks and groans of a shipyard at rest. Often the setting sun painted the sky a brilliant red, treating the shipwrights to a magnificent view and cheering their hearts, for they all knew and believed that famous seamen's proverb: "Red sky at night, sailor's delight." For them the red tinged evening sky foretold fair weather, good fortune and a promising new workday.

Shipsmith, M. "Kelly" Kellam works her magic with fire, muscle, skill and white-hot iron.

As light gave way to dark, the shipwrights carefully cleaned, sharpened and stowed their tools, leaving the little shipyard still and quiet in the moonlight. Soon the workday cycle would start again, and the dawn of a new day would signal the resumption of the concert that would not end until a new tall ship was launched.

One of the first things to be done was to make a full-scale drawing of every part of the ship so that patterns could be made and the great timbers cut, shaped and fit together. This is a time-honored process, called lofting, where the line drawings prepared by a naval architect are reproduced as full-scale lines, usually on the floor of a large building. Lofting for the new Kalmar Nyckel took place in the shipyard's sail loft, the only building large enough for the job. The sail loft's plywood floor was painted white to serve as a giant canvas for the full-scale lines of the ship. When patterns had been made from the lofted lines, a new plywood floor was put down over the lofting floor to preserve the lines in case they were needed in the future.

The greenheart keel was laid in April 1995. The sternpost was stepped in June, and shipwrights erected the first of some thirty-five frames on March 29, 1996. Each frame was made of about ten curved and hand-fit pieces called futtocks. By midyear 1997 the hull framing was completed, and the big pile of wood was much smaller. The huge hull timbers had all been sawn and hand-shaped to fit together perfectly like pieces of a giant jigsaw puzzle. Each piece of the puzzle was fastened in place with bolts and trunnels, or treenails made entirely of wood.

Meanwhile, iron bars were transformed into hinges, nails, straps, hooks, eyes and rings by a lady blacksmith using the shipyard's forge, anvils, mallets and tongs. Black smoke billowed every day from the blacksmith's shed as iron bars were heated and made ready for shaping with hammer, anvil, muscle and skill. There was a brilliant shower of sparks, like fireflies on a summer's evening, each time the blacksmith struck the white-hot iron with her hammer. The sound of metal on metal filled the air along with the sounds of the shipwright's hammers, saws, chisels and planes. There were other sounds, too, as sail makers, wood carvers and riggers added their notes to the symphony of wooden shipbuilding.

Each of the ship's great frames are made of about ten curved and hand-fit pieces called futtocks. When planked these frames will form the Kalmar Nyckel's graceful hull.

Next the hull was planked with two-inch thick locust. Each plank was hand-fit to its fore and aft neighbor using scarf joints. Once fit and hewed to shape, the planks were steamed in a handmade steam box at one hour for each inch of thickness, carried aloft hot, bent to shape, clamped in place and secured with trunnel and bolt. It was hot, hard work, and it took many hands to lift and position the heavy, steam-heated planks. Soon, however, the crew could see and feel the fair and graceful lines of the ship as they worked together in port and starboard side hull-planking teams. There soon developed some friendly competition between teams as to which could cut, fit, steam, clamp and bolt in place the most planks in a day.

When the very last hull plank, called the shutter plank, was ready to be hammered in place with a golden spike, the master shipbuilder called for the traditional shutter plank celebration. Volunteers and shipwrights, invited guests and the public came to be a part of this milestone and to share their pride in the results of the work so far. Each member of the building crew proudly signed his or her name on the shutter plank and took turns pounding the golden spike with a heavy hammer. It was happy work and everyone cheered when the last blow was struck.

The dream was now almost a boat — at least it started to look like a boat! Each day more and more people visited the shipyard to watch the progress, and more craftsmen came to help — timber framers, joiners, cabinet makers, master carpenters, wood carvers and caulkers.

As planking progressed the crew could see and feel the fair and graceful lines of the ship. Here a shipwright uses a slick to fair a hull timber.

Work now shifted to the rigging, the masts and yards, the decking, the fine joinery and finish details, the decorative carving, the caulking and finally the painting and preparation for launch. The end was almost in sight, and everyone in the little shipyard looked forward to the day the ship would be launched. That long-awaited day would be the true test of everyone's skill and dedication.

A beautiful tall ship was taking shape before everyone's eyes. Each new day brought changes, and soon the scaffolding that encased the emerging ship would be taken down, leaving the results of the building crews' efforts standing alone and proud in her cradle, much like a giant butterfly fresh from its cocoon.

A beautiful tall ship begins to emerge from it's scaffolding as a shipwright prepares to hoist the sprit top to its place on the bow sprit.

Huge masts and yards that support the ship's sails were being readied in various parts of the shipyard. Under the eves of the sail loft long, straight Douglas and Sitka fir timbers were shaped by hand plane from four to eight to sixteen to thirty-two sides. Finally, they were planed from thirty-two sides to round and tapered to form the ship's three big masts (fore, main and mizzen), the bowsprit, eight yards and various spars and flagstaffs.

Each of the three masts as well as the bowsprit supports two sails. A total of nearly 6,800 square feet of sail area drives the ship at nine to twelve knots under full sail and with a fair wind. The two bowsprit sails, the sprit and sprit topsail, give the new Kalmar Nyckel a very distinct profile like no other American-owned tall ship.

The masts and bowsprit also have large, round platforms called tops. These serve several purposes. They provide access to the topmasts, make a convenient platform to work on the ship's rigging and running gear and, when needed, can be used as part of the ship's defense system. When used for defense, they were called "fighting tops," and they gave sharpshooters stationed there with muskets a wide, unobstructed field of fire on the decks and rigging of enemy ships.

There was little doubt that the master shipbuilder and his crew had the skill, knowledge and experience to get the job done, but it was another story when it came to the Kalmar Nyckel's wood carvings. Everyone from the architect to the master shipbuilder himself had some doubt as to whether the skill needed to duplicate seventeenth-century Dutch woodcarvings existed in twentieth-century Delaware.

At first one or two people who had done some carving of decoys and other home hobby projects using knives and sandpaper expressed an interest in testing their skill on larger projects using mallets and chisels. Much to the relief of the master shipbuilder word of the need for woodcarvers spread among members of a local woodcarving group, and soon a few more hobbyists volunteered to try their hand at seventeenth-century carving.

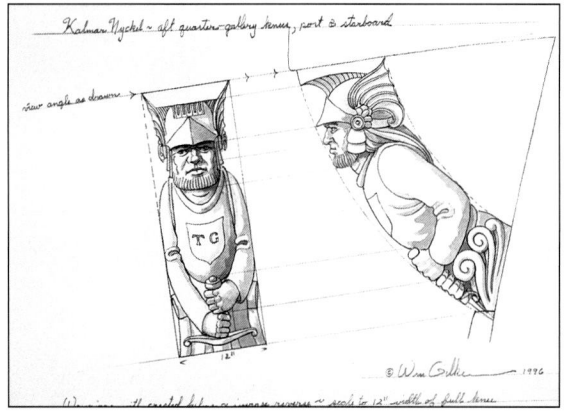

Eventually ten wood carvers, mostly local volunteers, worked from drawings of seventeenth-century ship decorations to create griffins, lions, soldiers, wind gods, dolphins, mermaids, mermen, birds, sea monsters, emblems, crowns, maidens, leaves, carved rope patterns, keys, angels and more—all representative of the type of carving that would have graced the original Kalmar Nyckel.

Ships of the seventeenth-century were very ornate and the new Kalmar Nyckel would be too! Wood carvers used the same mallets, chisels, planes, handsaws, rasps and scrapers the Dutch carvers of the 1620s used to make the carvings for the original Kalmar Nyckel. The carver's skilled hands turned knees into eagles and pelicans. Bitts became griffins, maidenheads, knightheads or carved rope knots called turks' heads. An eight-foot, two-tailed lion became the figurehead, and the transom was covered with mermaids, mermen, emblems, sea creatures, dolphins, lions, soldiers, wind gods and portraits of important people.

The ship's great cabin has four carved knees, each of a different mythological figure, an ornate settee, and window and door trim decorations befitting the master of a grand ship.

The ornate settee in the great cabin is dominated by two golden beasts carved in mahogany. The beasts are mythological creatures called griffins.

Architects drawings guided the skilled hands of carver/shipwright Jim Knowles who sculpted these figures in western red cedar for the ship's quarter gallery.

The Kalmar Nyckel griffins were patterned after those found on the stern crest sculpture of Sweden's famous warship Vasa. Built in the mid-1620s at the Royal Shipyard in Stockholm, Sweden, as Gustav II Adolf's warship, the Vasa met with disaster on her August 1628 maiden voyage. As the royal warship got underway, she was an impressive sight, indeed. She was one of Europe's largest and most ornate ships with two massive gun decks sprouting sixty-four cannons.

About two hours into her maiden voyage, the Vasa was overcome by strong gusts of wind and was twice heeled dangerously to port. The second strong gust heeled her so far to port that she began taking on water through her lower gun ports. With "full sail and all flags flying," as reported in Sweden's Royal Council account of the disaster, the Vasa went to the bottom of Stockholm's harbor in 105 feet of cold, dark water.

Vasa's story did not end with her untimely sinking, for in April 1961, after 333 years in the mud of the harbor bottom, the Vasa was raised. Amazingly,

Vasa-style griffins adorn the captain's ornate settee, perhaps the first such beasts carved for a wooden tall ship since the mid-1620s.

her hull was virtually intact, and her ornate wooden sculptures were well preserved by the mud that covered them. The great ship has since been restored to near-original glory and is on display in Sweden.

The Vasa is perhaps the most important example of seventeenth-century ship building and ornamental carving in the world today. She was literally covered with wooden sculptures. Some 490 intricate sculpted figures and nearly 200 lesser ornaments have been recovered, many so well preserved that they still had traces of their original paint and gilding. One of the most important and impressive Vasa sculptures was the stern crest carving of two

Carver Lyt Patterson uses mallet, chisel and skill to shape one of the Kalmar Nyckel's many ornate wooden sculptures.

magnificent griffins holding a crown over the likeness of a young Gustav Adolf.

Since ancient times the fabled griffin has been a popular symbol of royalty, power and authority. Griffins have always been portrayed as a cross between an eagle and a lion, with the head, upper body and front legs of an eagle and the lower body and hind legs of a lion, including claws and a long, tufted tail. The Vasa griffins, however, have two important differences making them unique among griffins. The Vasa carvers gave their griffins short tails and cloven hooves for hind feet. So it seemed proper for the Kalmar Nyckel carvers to follow the lead of the Vasa carvers in recreating the Vasa griffins for the captain's settee and in so doing creating yet another link to Sweden's proud past. Interestingly, the Kalmar Nyckel's settee griffins could very well be the first Vasa-style griffins carved for a wooden tall ship since the Vasa's carvers took up their mallets and chisels over three centuries ago.

Many of the ship's carvings reflect the historic ties between the cities of Kalmar, Sweden, and Wilmington, Delaware. There are symbols of Sweden, America, Delaware, Kalmar and Wilmington all around the ship. They take the form of city, state and country seals and symbols such as the Delaware state tree (American holly) and insect (lady bug), the Swedish crown and the blue and gold colors of both Sweden and Delaware.

As the carvers made great mounds of wood chips with sharp chisels and flying mallets, they too became part of the growing symphony of sights and sounds along the banks of the Christina River. Soon new notes would be heard as the ship's hull and deck planks were made ready for caulking to make the ship watertight and seaworthy.

The ship's figurehead will get a coat of red paint to match the color of seventeenth-century Swedish lion sculptures before it takes it's place of honor at the bow.

Two caulkers from Boston, Massachusetts, arrived at the shipyard with the tools of their craft: caulking irons, caulking mallets, rave hooks, cotton, oakum and tar. Now the symphony was in full voice! The shipyard rang with the rhythmic tapping of the caulkers, the crisp shaving of planes drawn along the masts by shipwrights, the mallet blows and chisels of carvers, the ring of the shipsmith's anvil, the thud of trunnels driven home, the buzz of the carpenter's saws and the voices of proud workers on a mission.

The caulkers pounded and packed the hull and deck seams with cotton, then oakum and tar or, in some cases, a more modern seam compound. They did their job so well that after the ship was launched, the lead caulker reported to the master shipbuilder on the status of his hurried inspection of the bilge and said with obvious pride and satisfaction, not to mention a bit of relief, "There is not enough water to make a cup of tea." That meant the seams were tight even before the hull planking had a chance to swell and make the seams even tighter. It was a caulker's dream come true: a tight ship and a job well done! It also caused the master shipbuilder to smile broadly and sigh with relief. One more worry behind him!

While the hull and deck were being sealed, the ship's eight sails were being finished in Maine, and more than eight miles of rope were being fashioned into the standing and running rigging needed to support the masts and help sail the ship.

Caulker Joe Chetwynd, "Joe DeCaulka", works on sealing the hull seams with cotton and oakum. This ancient craft is critical to making a vessel watertight and seaworthy.

Four cannons and two rail guns were cast in an Indiana foundry and delivered to the shipyard, awaiting the completion of wooden carriages and handmade ironwork from the blacksmith's forge. The four big cannons (two six-pound and two three-pound) each have a seventeenth-century-style raised crest on the barrel that was hand sculpted by a local sculptor/carver and made a part of the casting. Cannons are classified by the size of the cannonball they fire. A three-pound cannon fires a three-pound ball, a six-pound cannon a six-pound ball, etc.

Another milestone celebration took place in August 1997 when the ship's graceful bow was dedicated and the lion figurehead was publicly unveiled for the first time. Again hundreds gathered and filled the little shipyard. Mayors, governors and community leaders joined the festivities, made speeches and marveled at the great red figurehead that was over a year in the making. The lion was painted red to match seventeenth-century Swedish lions, and he had two tails so a tail could be seen from either side of the bow. The proud carver was introduced, and his work was loudly applauded and cheered by an admiring crowd.

This time there was no mistaking it! Before them stood a beautiful ship nearly ready to meet her true element for the very first time—the sea! For the new Kalmar Nyckel, however, it would first be the tidal waters of her Christina River home, then the Delaware or Chesapeake Bay to the Atlantic Ocean and the open sea.

With final launch preparations moving ahead at an ever more feverish pace, master carpenters and cabinet makers made railings, spiral stairs leading from the quarter deck to the main deck and below, and the great cabin furnishings. Others finished the windlass, the capstan, the anchors, cathead, gun ports, scuppers and binnacle. The whipstaff, tiller and rudder by which the ship is steered came next. Still other artisans fashioned the capstan and windlass bars and the ship's hatch covers. Leaded glass gallery windows were made, and the roofs of the quarter gallery windows were sheathed in brilliant new handmade copper shingles. Volunteers painted, oiled and polished above the

The Kalmar Nyckel's eight-foot, two-tailed, red lion figurehead was over a year in the making by volunteer carver, Roger Hone.

waterline and artists brought the ship's carvings to life with authentic, bright seventeenth-century colors. The big day was getting closer and closer!

Now the work was almost nonstop as the countdown to launch was on! Finally, the hull received several coats of paint, and house movers slowly and ever so carefully positioned the great ship securely on her ways, a move of some forty feet from where she had waited since her keel was laid so many months ago. Everyone in the shipyard turned out to see the ship being moved to the specially made steel launching ways. They were very proud and more than a little relieved when the ship was safely in place. This had been an anxious moment, but all was well and the long anticipated launch was only a matter of hours away! As night fell on September 27, 1997, the shipyard lay peaceful and quiet in the moonlight — waiting, waiting, waiting for the first signs of a glorious, new day dawning — launch day.

During almost two and a half years of building, thousands of people had joined the dream. On September 28 they gathered on the banks of the Christina River and filled the little shipyard to overflowing. They had come to see the dream, now their dream too, poised on her ways waiting patiently to be launched.

Bands played, flags fluttered in the light breeze and bright sunshine, cannons fired, fire boats sprayed water high in the air in graceful rainbow-colored arcs, mayors, governors, ambassadors and representatives of four nations spoke; and the people clapped, cheered, cried and cheered again. It was a very exciting time for everyone.

At exactly high tide, her land tethers were cut, and the dream gracefully slid sternfirst into the Christina River. With hardly a ripple the new Kalmar Nyckel settled at her mooring at the very spot her predecessor anchored nearly 360 years before. At the moment she floated free of the land, trailing her mooring lines, there was a mighty roar that all but drowned out the

Bands played, flags fluttered, cannons roared, fire boats sprayed water high in the air and people cheered, cried and cheered again. It was a grand and glorious, proud and emotional launch day

cheering crowd. She had fired her very first cannon salute from her flag-draped deck. Fire and smoke belched from the muzzle of her six-pound cannon and drifted lazily across the river to the delight of everyone, and all the boats gathered to welcome Delaware's tall ship, Kalmar Nyckel!

Her salute was answered by a shore battery cannonade and the toots, whistles and cannons of the welcoming flotilla. For the building crew, which had been so close to her for so many months, it was a bittersweet moment. Throats tightened and eyes filled, but that soon gave way to big smiles, handshakes and backslaps all around as volunteers, shipwrights and artisans of all the crafts needed to build the ship celebrated their handiwork. The crew gathered on deck around the capstan to take part in a centuries-old custom. Manning the capstan bars, they took turns slowly turning the capstan while a maiden, perched atop its lead crown, played sea chanteys on a violin.

It was a wonderful, proud, joyous and, just a little, sad day! For it was both a beginning and an end. A beginning of the next chapter for the ship and an end to the building of a dream and the family of men and women who gave so much of themselves to bring the dream to life. This group of dedicated volunteers and craftspeople, now true workmates, would soon move on to help fulfill other dreams being dreamed in other places like Ireland, Connecticut, Maryland and California. Wherever there are dreams, dream-builders will follow.

The Kalmar Nyckel was reborn and afloat again! With her rebirth a new vision and dream about her future mission as Delaware's tall ship ambassador was launched. That dream continues today!

Often when we dream really good dreams, we wake to find they were just that: really good dreams. This time though, thanks to the vision, skill, talent, dedication and unconditional love of volunteers and artisans alike, the dream was real!

Captain David Hiott, master of the Kalmar Nyckel, is poised to sail Delaware's tall ship ambassador into the future.

Tall ships take on personalities of their own, and those fortunate enough to build and sail them soon realize that they are much more than the materials from which they are made. They seem to have hearts and souls that invite perfection, loyalty and love and that reward seamanship, craftsmanship and loving care. They please the eye, stir the emotion, fire the imagination and lift the spirit. They are the white-winged angels of the sea. Without them and the men and women who built and sailed them, the world would most certainly be a different and far less satisfying place.

MAY GOD BLESS THE KALMAR NYCKEL
AND ALL WHO SAIL WITH HER.

Launch day christening prayer
Martha Carper
September 28, 1997

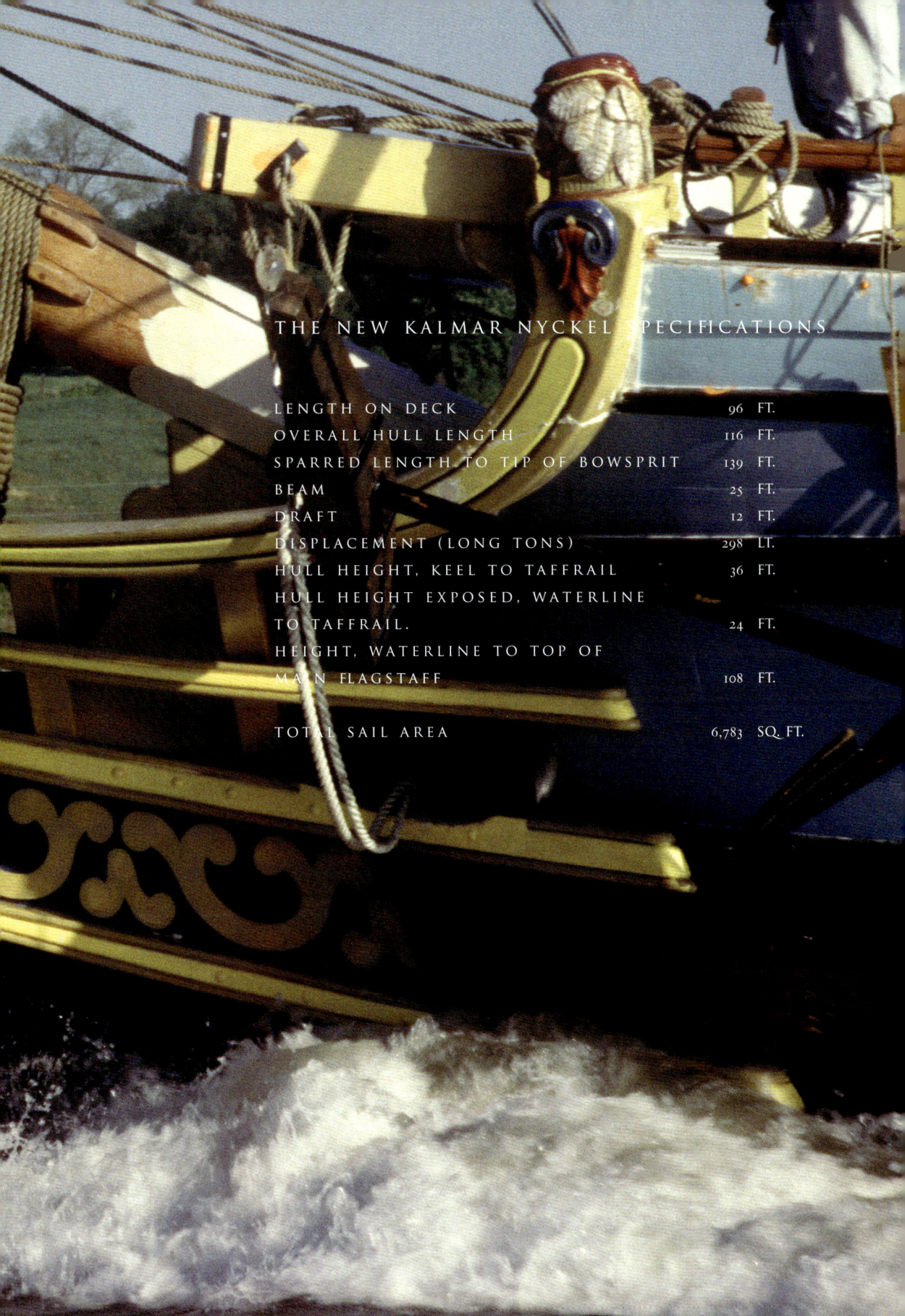

THE NEW KALMAR NYCKEL SPECIFICATIONS

LENGTH ON DECK	96 FT.
OVERALL HULL LENGTH	116 FT.
SPARRED LENGTH TO TIP OF BOWSPRIT	139 FT.
BEAM	25 FT.
DRAFT	12 FT.
DISPLACEMENT (LONG TONS)	298 LT.
HULL HEIGHT, KEEL TO TAFFRAIL	36 FT.
HULL HEIGHT EXPOSED, WATERLINE TO TAFFRAIL.	24 FT.
HEIGHT, WATERLINE TO TOP OF MAIN FLAGSTAFF	108 FT.
TOTAL SAIL AREA	6,783 SQ. FT.

GLOSSARY

Aft or Abaft
To the rear of. Toward the stern.

Aloft
Above the deck of a ship. Upwards as in "carried up into the scaffolding surrounding the ship during construction."

Anvil
Iron or steel block on which metal objects are hammered into shape. Part of a blacksmith's arsenal of tools.

Beam
Width of a ship at its widest.

Below
Below the main deck of a ship.

Bilge
The lowest part of a ship's hull or hold.

Binnicle
Case enclosing a ship's compass, usually near the helm.

Bitt
Any of a ship's deck posts, often in pairs and sometimes ornately carved, around which rope is wound and held fast.

Block
A mechanical device consisting of one or more pulleys. Used to transmit power or direction by means of a rope passing around the pulley.

Bow
Front or forward end of a ship.

Bowsprit
The spar projecting forward from the bow of a ship from which sails are set.

Capstan
A cylinder on deck that revolves on its vertical axis to provide mechanical advantage when seamen push against bars inserted in its head. Used for heavy jobs such as weighing anchor, hoisting yards or raising and lowering top masts.

Cathead
A structure or heavy timber at the bow of a ship used for lifting anchors on board. Seamen often carved a cat head on the end of the timber.

Caulk
To fill or seal a crack or joint.

Caulker
One who caulks ships.

Chantey
A song that sailors sing in rhythm with their work.

Chock
A block secured to the deck near the capstan that serves to break or stop and lock the capstan's motion.

Draft
The depth of water that a ship displaces.

Fair
Smooth and even. Said of a ship's lines, a well-fit joint or a perfectly planed spar.

Fairlead
A block of wood (or metal) with holes through which lines may be led clearly and unobstructed, to their final destination.

Figurehead
An important woodcarving mounted at the bow of a ship.

Fish oil
A liquid wood preservative made from fish, usually menhaden.

Fore
Forward or toward the bow of a ship.

Futtocks
Any of the upright, curved timbers forming the ribs of a wooden ship.

Griffin
A mythical animal with the body and hind legs of a lion and the head and wings of an eagle. The griffins on the Kalmar Nyckel's great cabin settee have the body and front legs of a lion and the hind legs of a cloven-hoofed beast, copied from carvings found on the seventeenth-century Swedish warship Vasa.

Joiner
A carpenter who finishes interior woodwork such as doors, molding, stairs, etc. His trade or skill is called joinery.

Knee
Naturally grown or laminated wood in the shape of a bent knee, used as a structural brace.

Long ton
Unit of weight equal to 2,240 pounds.

Oakum
Hemp or jute fiber used for caulking seams in wooden ships.

Pinnace
A classification or type of ship. Dutch pinnace refers to wooden vessels with three masts, a flat transom and square rig, built in Holland.

Port
Left-hand side of a ship when facing forward.

Quarter deck
The after part of the upper deck of a ship, usually reserved for officers.

Rigger
A person whose work is making and fitting the rope and gear that support and operate the masts, yards and sails of a ship.

Rudder
A flat, finlike piece of wood hinged vertically from the stern of a ship, used for steering.

Running rigging
All moveable lines and blocks (or pulleys) by which the top masts and sails are set and controlled.

Scarf
A joint made by notching, grooving or cutting the ends of two timbers and fastening them so they lap and join firmly into one continuous piece.

Scuppers
Shallow, gutterlike depression around the edge of a ship's deck and the holes through which water drains from the deck.

Settee
A seat or bench with a back, usually large enough for two or three people.

Shipwright
A person whose work is the building and repair of ships.

Spar
Any pole on a ship.

Standing rigging
All the generally fixed lines and chains by which the masts are secured and braced.

Starboard
Right-hand side of a ship when facing forward.

Step
Raised frame or platform supporting the sternpost or butt end of a mast.

Stern
The back or aft end of a ship.

Sternpost
The main upright piece at the stern of a ship, usually supporting the rudder.

Taffrail
The rail at the stern of a ship.

Tiller
A bar or handle for turning a ship's rudder. The Kalmar Nyckel is steered by a bar connected to the tiller called a whipstaff.

Timber framer
A woodworker who builds frames for a structure and joins timbers by means of notched joints and wooden pegs or treenails.

Transom
Any of the crossbeams attached to the sternpost of a wooden ship. The Kalmar Nyckel's transom is flat, high and ornately decorated with woodcarvings and a gallery.

Trunnel
A wooden peg or treenail used to fasten timbers together.

Ways
A timber or steel framework on which a ship is built and/or from which it slides at launching.

Whipstaff
The helmsman's bar by which the Kalmar Nyckel is steered. Attached to the tiller and rudder, it is moved by the helmsman to right or left to turn the ship to starboard or port.

Windlass
A horizontal deck winch used to provide mechanical advantage in lifting or hauling heavy objects such as yards, top masts and anchors. Turned by means of bars inserted in its cylinder and heaved around by seamen.

Yard
A horizontal spar of wood (or metal) that supports a sail. Usually tapered at the ends and fastened at right angles across a mast.

58

MALLETS, CHISELS & PLANES

HAND TOOLS THEN AND NOW

The art of wooden-boat building is timeless. So too are many of the hand tools used to build boats of wood. The very same hand tools used in the 1600s are still used today. In fact, if a seventeenth-century carver, caulker or shipwright visited a twenty-first century wooden boat shipyard, he or she would feel right at home with many of the tools of the trade. Carvers, caulkers, riggers, sail makers and shipwrights all had special tools. Each tool was designed for a purpose and to get the results the user wanted. Workmen and sailors often made their own tools out of scrap material found on board ship or in the shipyard. Unlike home building, there are few if any straight lines or right angles on a boat. Almost everything is curved. Fitting pieces together required skill and special tools.

By themselves tools are just objects, but in the hand of an artisan (shipwright, carver, rigger, caulker, sail maker, blacksmith) they are an extension of the user's hand and skill. Hand tools are to the artisan as brush and canvas are to the artist.

The early shipbuilders not only built great ships of wood but also designed and made tools that served their needs so well that they survived hundreds of years with few if any changes. Their ships, their tools and their skills are a priceless legacy.

Here a few of the early boat builder's tools that are still used today:

CARVERS
Mallet
Made of hard wood and used to strike a chisel in order to shape wood. Often handmade from shipyard scrap.

Chisel
A very sharp, hard metal blade with a wooden handle. Used to shape wood. Can be struck with a mallet or pushed by hand. Made in a variety of shapes for special cuts. Often handmade from shipyard scrap.

CAULKERS

Mallet
Used to strike caulking irons that drive cotton and oakum into seams between planks of wooden boats to make them watertight. Often handmade by caulkers.

Caulking iron
Metal wedges used to drive cotton and oakum into seams to make them watertight. Struck with a caulkers mallet. Hand struck by the shipyard blacksmith.

Rave hook
A hooked iron bar used to clean out old caulking from seams. Handmade by the shipyard blacksmith.

RIGGERS

Marline spike
A pointed metal or wooden spike for separating strands of a rope. Usually handmade.

SAILMAKERS

Needle
Heavy needle for stitching or repairing canvas sails.

Palm
A metal disk used over the palm of the hand to push a needle through canvas.

SHIPWRIGHTS

Box plane
A chisel blade mounted by means of a wooden wedge in a block of wood. Usually handmade. Used to level, smooth and remove wood.

Square
A ninety degree angle made of wood, metal or wood and metal. Used to lay out or test right angles. Often handmade.

Bevel square
A rule with a movable arm used to measure or mark angles. Often handmade.

Batten
A handmade, thin and flexible strip of wood used to measure or mark curves.

Saw
A toothed metal blade pushed and pulled by hand to cut wood.

Slick
A large flat-bladed chisel used to shape and fit wood. Pushed using arms and upper body. Often handmade.

Adze
A metal blade at right angles to a wooden handle used to shape wood.

Axe
A wooden-handled sharp metal blade for chopping, splitting and shaping wood.

Awl
A small pointed tool for making holes in wood or leather. Also used to transfer patterns to wood by means of punching small holes along the lines of a pattern.

Scraper
A metal shape burnished to a wire edge and used to smooth wood. Often handmade.

Scribe
A pointed metal instrument for marking a line on wood. Often handmade.

TRIBUTE TO HAND TOOLS

FROM THE BOOK SKETCHES OF AMERICA PAST BY ERIC SLOANE

"Most of today's tools have a cheapness of mass production; the old hand-made tools often had design that made them examples of fine art. When you hold an early implement, when you close your hand over the worn wooden handle, you know exactly how it felt to the craftsman whose hand had smoothed it to its rich patina. In that instant you are as close to that craftsman as you can be… In that moment you are near to another being in another life, and you are that much richer."

The heft and feel of a well-worn handle,
The sight of shavings that curl from a blade;
The logs in the woodpile, the sentiment of huge beams in an old-fashioned house;
The smell of fresh cut timber and the pungent fragrance of burning leaves;
The crackle of kindling and hiss of burning logs.
Abundant to all the needs of man, how poor the world would be
Without wood.

Everard Hinrichs

ACKNOWLEDGEMENTS

For a novice writer a book project can be a daunting undertaking indeed. What started as a diversion from boredom on a rainy beach weekend soon became a formidable challenge. Getting thoughts on paper is easy and fun. Then comes the tedious process of editing, rewriting, tweaking and trying to get published. "How To" books for dummies are helpful but no substitute for talented, supportive and knowledgeable people. I was fortunate to have more than a handful of these on which to lean heavily.

Family and friends can always be counted on for support and encouragement but there are many others that contribute importantly; neighbors, published authors, graphic designers, photographers, educators and historians.

Neighbor, Catherine Tracy provided early training in the use of such basic PC skills as cut, paste, page up and page down. Without these elementary navigation skills the manuscript would no doubt still be scribbled in longhand and stuffed away in some forgotten drawer. From that humble start a team of people provided advice, constructive criticism, encouragement, support and a strong measure of optimistic enthusiasm for which I am most greatful. Among them are Judyth Holton, teacher, The Independence School, Captain David Hiott, Master of the Kalmar Nyckel, Steve Luthultz, Executive Director, Kalmar Nyckel Foundation, Claudia Young and Nancy Carol Willis, Delaware authors, Deborah Haskell, Delaware Heritage Commission, and photographer, Chris Queeney. Two others deserve special mention for their tireless and enthusiastic support from the start. They are Kim Burdick, Burdick Associates and Christine Celano, graphic designer. Without Kim and Christine the project would not have made it past that rainy beach weekend.

Finally, I owe special thanks to friends and master shipbuilders Allen and Liz Rawl who not only gave me the opportunity and privilege of working as a volunteer wood carver and member of the Kalmar Nyckel building crew, but offered encouragement and technical editing support while fully engaged in yet another wooden boat building project in California. Without this team and the skilled craftsmen and women who worked on the Kalmar Nyckel, the ship and this book would not exist. Thank you all!